Chû nnâna 202 nì Chû Mǐŋgâkà bô Jǐŋglîshì

Chû Nnâna 202 nì Chû Mìŋgâkà bô Jìŋglîshì

202 PROVERBS IN MUNGAKA AND ENGLISH

Second Edition

❧

Alfred Willibroad Daiga

Edited by
Emma Yeluma Daiga

SPEARS Ⓢ BOOKS
DENVER, COLORADO

Spears Books
An Imprint of Spears Media Press LLC
7830 W. Alameda Ave, Suite 103-247
Denver, CO 80226
United States of America

First Published in the United States of America in 2023 by Spears Books
www.spearsbooks.org
info@spearsmedia.com
Information on this title: www.spearsbooks.org/202-proverbs-in-Mungaka-and-English

First Edition published in May 1994, Yaounde, Cameroon

ISBN: 9781957296203 (Paperback)
ISBN: 9781957296210 (eBook)

Spears Media Press has no responsibility for the persistence or accuracy of urls for external or third-party internet websites referred to in this publication, and does not guarantee that any content on such websites is, or will remain, accurate or appropriate.

Designed and typeset by Spears Media Press LLC
Cover designed by DKK
Cover Art: Daimond D; it illustrates the proverb - mĭ mbam sɨŋ, ŋgɔb ŋku (feeding the birds of the air and starving the chickens at home).

Distributed globally by African Books Collective (ABC)
www.africanbookscollective.com

Dedication

To my mother, who stood by us after the death of our father

In remembrance of My Dad
Hon A.W. Daiga (of Blessed Memory)
GREEN & WHITE

Green and White
On the Cover
Is not by chance,
My dad,
Hon. A.W. Daiga
Did admire
Those two colours,
Green and white,

I remember once
When the inside of our house
Ceiling and walls,
Benches and stools
Window shutters and doors
Cushion covers and tablecloths
Were in all
Green and white

Green signifies peace
White, plain truth
'Tis known that
Those who love and promote
Peace, truth and unity
Admire

Green and white

My dad
Hon. A.W. Daiga
When he had to work with paint
It was always
Green and white.

Emma Yeluma Daiga
Yaounde, May 1994

Contents

FOREWORD TO THE FIRST EDITION

Proverbs abound in every culture. In Ibo society, Chinua Achebe writes, "Proverbs are the palm oil with which words are eaten." The use of proverbs is universal and transcends the concern of sociolinguists and other researchers.

My involvement with this project springs from a strong attachment to my culture, its transmission and propagation. It is therefore not unconnected to Ma Emma's original idea of a publication of this nature; that is, to encourage those who are interested in learning and communicating in proverbs, as well as immortalise a man, Hon. A.W. Daiga, her father, whose life and works were never divorced from the indigenous culture of his people.

Of significant value to me is the modesty and sincerity behind this work. Suggestions to consult technical and expert opinions have been absorbed to some degree. The need for a thematic and structural classification of the proverbs has been retained for future editions. The overriding principle in the project was to publish the proverbs as they were originally collected. This work is therefore neither a linguistic document nor an academic exercise. It is a cultural document meant to enhance the learning and use of proverbs in the process of cultural transmission and propagation.

Language is dynamic. Most of the proverbs, however, maintain their original meaning except perhaps in situations and contexts where the translations are made to accommodate new ideas and experiences that reflect the universality of thought in language

No work of this nature can lay claims to perfection, given man's imperfect nature and the possibility of error in a collective endeavour. The reader may likely come across some that will affect meaning and usage both in Mungaka and in English. This work, therefore should stimulate interest in the collection and use of proverbs in Mungaka as well as provoke thought, debate and criticism on the codification, standardisation and teaching of Mungaka. I salute other publications in this area, especially the Mungaka (Bali) Dictionary.

It is time we moved from a consumers' culture to that of production and propagation of sound values, we are open to suggestions and criticisms.

Kwasen Gwangwa'a

PRAISE FOR THE FIRST EDITION

This collection of proverbs drawn from the folklore of the Bali Nyonga comes on the heels of many publications that have recently come to light about Bali culture by native and expatriate scholars. It indicates the ever-growing interest writers have shown and continue to show in the dynamism of a unique ethnic group with a two-century-old history marked by chivalry and conquest.

The proverbs testify to the migratory trajectory of the Chamba from their motherland in the plains of the Adamawa mountain ranges southward through the Tikar regions and the Bamelike grasslands to their present site in the southwest of the Bamenda Grassfields - a trajectory fraught with danger, resistance and wars which in turn spurned a culture of conciliation, human dignity and statesmanship.

Established in about the 1840s under the leadership of Fonyonga I, Bali Nyonga proceeded to build one of the most advanced city-states in the Grassfields. The earliest literature about the Bali Nyonga dates to 1916 when Dr. Adolph Vilhauer of the Basel Mission printed on the mission hand press at Fumban, the first volume of a grammatical description of Mungaka, the language of Bali Nyonga.

The literature ever since has steadily increased, and the present collection is just another drop in the ocean which it is hoped would provide a wider exploratory field for cultural amateurs and experts.

Sam-Nuvala Fonkem

ACKNOWLEDGMENT

Many thanks to my friend Mademoiselle Paraiso Nielle my first hostess and very good friend in Paris, who first typed this work in Mungaka and arranged it in a booklet form.

THE MAKING OF CHÛ NNÂNA - FIRST EDITION

Before leaving for Paris (France) for training in 'Haute Cou-
ture' (fashion design) in 1978, I tried to put some order in
the Daiga Family Library in Bali. While doing this work, I came
across an envelope with 202 pieces of paper, and each of them
had a proverb in Mungaka.

While travelling to Paris I took these proverbs with me.
Around early 1979, my friend and hostess Nielle Paraiso, a Beni-
noise who understood not a single word in English or Mungaka,
typed out the proverbs and arranged them in a booklet form.
She used a French keyboard and put the accents manually. We
made five sample copies. On my return to Cameroon in December 1979, I looked for someone to translate these proverbs into
English. One Mr Dan Forje who was postmaster at the time in
Bali Nyonga, volunteered to do the job and up to this moment
that I am writing, Mr Forje has neither brought back the translation nor the booklet of proverbs in Mungaka. My intention to
translate this work earlier was to have it before July 1982, which
was the tenth anniversary of my father's death.

In May 1982 I got news that my brother's wife, Bosen Grace
Gwanyalla Daiga, who was so dear to me had died. I rushed
back to Cameroon. During my stay in Cameroon, I followed up
with Mr. Dan Forje to get the Mungaka manuscript all in vain.

I went to Paris and finally returned in 1983. Sometime in
1984, my elder brother, Dinga and I attempted to translate the

proverb into English but did not succeed. We did just a few. After all the attempts, I decided to publish the proverb in Mungaka only. Around April 1990, I took it to the University of Lagos for publishing but Ni Peter Kehdinga Fogam, lecturer in the Law Faculty of the University of Lagos advised me to do the translations into English before publishing.

In September 1990, I gave the proverbs to Mr. Gwangwa'a Gahlia of Pecten Cameroon Douala, who is a Mungaka writer. Three years later, in December 1990, I asked for them and got them without the translation due to his heavy workload at Pecten and frequent travels abroad.

Through my young friends Tina and Edwin Fongod, whom I was visiting one day in Douala, I met Mr. Njekoh Philip Fongod, talked about my work to him and he accepted to do the translations and took the work with him to Bali. That was in September 1993. About four weeks later, I got news in Lagos that the translation had been completed.

I obtained a one-week permission from my school in Lagos, Nigeria (where I am presently undertaking a course in African Textile and Fashion Design), to come back to Cameroon and give more assignments to volunteers on the work.

The very day I got to Douala, I met Mr. Fongod Edwin and gave him a theme to work on for this book; what he told me was: "Ma Emma, meet my friend Kwasen Gwangwa'a, ŋkɔŋ ŋwà'nì ì chə' nì yɔ̀ mbôm yum tì - *he has a sharp pen as far as this kind of work is concerned.*

After going to Bali and collecting the wonderful translations done by Mr. Njekoh Philip Fongod, I went straight to Yaounde and met Mr. Kwasen Gwangwa'a

It was one early morning on the 11th February 1994 that I got him up from bed. He spontaneously accepted my proposals and we sat on the work for the first time and worked for four hours drafting the body of the work. Before I returned to Lagos, I left the work with Mr. Kwasen Gwangwa'a, with a lot of confidence. He had the English translations, did more research, and contacted some of my family members like Ba Dinga Daiga, Doh

Daiga and Diane Daiga who furnished him with the information he needed.

By the time I returned from Lagos for a two-week vacation which I extended to a month in order to get this work through, Mr. Kwasen Gwangwa'a had come up with a more concrete overall draft.

We spent two days together going through the work he had done. While Dr. Margaret Awa Tita of E.N.S (Higher Teachers' Training School) Yaounde proofread the work, I took the Mungaka section to Bali Nyonga for typing.

Mr. Kwasen Gwangwa'a had directed me to Ni Victor Dohkea, a Mungaka computer specialist. He was quite willing to do the job but the computer at the Bali Fon's palace was faulty. We tried getting the Mungaka typewriter from the palace but could not lay our hands on it either.

After seeing persons like Mr. Philip Njekoh Fongod, the Mayor of Bali, Mr. Patrick Fosang and Raphael Forsi to get a Mungaka typewriter which I did not get, I gave up typing the work in Bali.

On the day I got offers from the mayor and Ni Raphael Forsi to use the ordinary machine, Ni Victor Dohkea was not around to do the work.

While doing the translation, Mr. Philip Fongod had noticed some errors in the Mungaka manuscript and called my attention to them. For that reason, with the help of Ni Victor Dohkea, I contacted Ba Fokom Sabe, a perfect Mungaka writer presently teaching at the Ntèd Nursery School, we immediately got the scripts and started work on them, there and then. When I told him goodbye that evening, he had corrected 45 proverbs. He did a lot of vital corrections especially putting the necessary accents and correcting some spellings. My mother, Mrs. Lucy Daiga helped a lot in explaining some of the proverbs, while Ni Victor Dohkea gave a chart of the Mungaka characters of the computer keyboard.

As soon as I returned to Yaounde, I went straight to Kwasen Gwangwa'a and gave him my report and we took off from there.

We contacted Miss Lela Sabina for typing on the computer. She directed me to Dr. Tangwa of the University of Yaounde I, who introduced his sister Tangwa Beri a computer specialist, to us. However, she could not do the job but sent us to Mr. Joe Nkwain of Polytech, another computer specialist. Mr. Nkwain and Dr. Bole Botake advised us to take the work to SIL (Société Internationale Linguistique) for it was their kind of job.

When we got to the SIL, we realised to our greatest surprise, that they could not produce all the characters of the Mungaka language. In fact, Mungaka, one of the first Cameroonian languages to be codified and written by European missionaries, does not even feature on the national language policy which SIL has developed for Cameroon. We were informed that what would be available on their computer program was what the government had decided.

They finally did the typing of the text without three Mungaka accents and another character which Kwasen and I added to the work manually.

The programme *Focus on Art*, a cultural programme on Cameroon Television CRTV, had always interested me while I was in Cameroon. It was one of my best programmes on TV. I should say I am lucky to have worked on this book with Mr. Kwasen Gwangwa'a, the producer of *Focus on Art*.

For the short time I worked with him, I discovered that he is very patient and serviceable. One Sunday afternoon, we went to look for a computer specialist whose house we did not know exactly. He was the third person we had to see that day. When we got to his former house, we had to wait for his neighbour who was not at home to return and direct us to the computer man's new house.

I was so impatient and discouraged, especially with the previous disappointments we had had, and wanted that we leave. Mr. K. Gwangwa'a asked me to be patient till the neighbour came. That bit of courage he gave me or piece of patience we exercised has opened the main way for these proverbs in Mungaka to be gotten on paper with the help of the computer. Before this time,

I attempted giving up several times and he kept encouraging me.

He damned the consequences and took me to people's houses as late as after midnight, woke up people from siesta, etc. all in the name of Chû Nnâna nì chû Mìŋgâkà. I cannot count the number of times I had to get him to forgo some of his appointments etc., which he accepted with smiles. He is a good person to work with.

I would like to encourage more Bali natives to bring up many more ideas to promote our culture through Kwasen Gwangwa'a's platform.

In the last days of the work, Kwasen and I were lucky to have one person whose contribution to the work was almost missed. Ni Sam-Nuvala Fonkem painstakingly went through the work, revising the translations to render them more accessible to readers. He also gave useful hints on the form of the book and its publishing.

In the course of the work, Kwasen Gwangwa'a, Dr. Margaret Tita, Gwanyalla Judith and Ba Dinga Daiga suggested that the proverbs be arranged in either alphabetical or thematic order. As said elsewhere, my intention was to publish these proverbs in a way and order of numbering my father left them.

Emma Yeluma Daiga

THE MAKING OF CHÛ NNÂNA -
SECOND EDITION

Knowing that Dr. Jude Fokwang teaches the Mungaka Language in our community, I contacted him to publish the second edition of Chû Nnâna. The question was how it would happen, as I did not have a copy of the first edition with me.

Leaving Bali Nyonga in 2017 for the US, my plan was to visit family for a few months and go back. I haven't been back until today and while travelling, I did not take a copy of the book because I had moved back to Cameroon with all my belongings after living in the US for a long time.

Mr. Charles Tamon and a host of others who knew about the book kept asking me for copies and that is how I seriously began to look for one around here. I could not ask my Siblings in Cameroon because they had all left Bali due to the ongoing crisis. My cousin, Dr. Tangeh Nicholas - ŋkɔm Gwanbidpua, had told me he saw a copy in a library in California. I googled and saw that a copy existed, edited by me and published by the University of California. I shared this information with Drs Lilian & Jude Fokwang and they were marvelled and encouraged me to press on.

Dr. Jude Fokwang had suspected that Dr. Sema Fofung might have a copy, and while planning to ask him, I called my brother, Bengyela Daiga, who had returned to reside in Bali. My brother had found a couple of copies that had been partially damaged. He spread them out in single pages and pressed them with a pressing iron. In the meantime, Dr. Fokwang had gotten Dr. Sema Fofung's copy and made photocopies.

When I followed up with my brother, he surprised me with a complete copy of the Mungaka version, all re-translated into the new Mungaka alphabet. The man behind this incredible work was Ni Pius Soja, aka Ba ma ŋkwa mbad, who had accomplished this feat as a birthday gift for my brother. All of this happened in 2021.

Dr. Fokwang being an expert in the Mungaka language, edited the Mungaka section. Goddy Gwaabe played a significant role in proofreading the book. My nephew, Doh Daiga, a young student at the time of the first edition, completed the illustration for the book. He now resides in Burkina Faso and has illustrated the artwork on the front cover.

Dr. Fokwang's colleague, Dr. Lilian Atanga, introduced us to a typist in Cameroon who typed the whole book in one day. This is how we were able to edit the remainder of the work and get it ready for publication. I am grateful to the following individuals for the invaluable role they have played towards the re-publication of this book: Mr. Bengyela Daiga, Dr. Sema Fofung, Dr. Fokwang, Goddy Gwaabe, Ni Pius Soja and Doh Daiga.

Emma Daiga,
November 6, 2023

Chû Nnâna 202 nì Chû Mìŋgâkà bô Jìŋglîshì

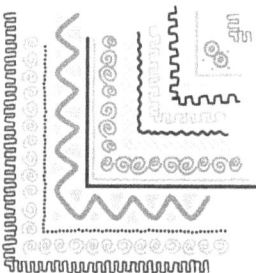

1. Mɨ̂, mɨ̀nchɨ̌nchì, Nɔ'ɨ ŋgɔ̀ŋ, ntɨ̂' ŋkwin ŋkaŋ.
   - Lɛ bə ŋgâ: N-nèbtî mɔ̌' yum kɛ̀ mɔ̌' fà', à bi bɔ̌ŋ, lɨ̀ŋ ta kàm.

2. À bɔ̌ŋ yù, mbâŋ-kɔ̌ŋ manjâm ù a.
   - Lɛ bə ŋgâ: Bî mùn bɛ̌ ni nsa' sa', bùn njamɨ ŋghemti bɔ̂ yɨ̌ ŋgàŋ-sa' lɛ, alɛ ù suŋ mbɔ̀ yɨ̌ ŋgàŋ-sa' bub.

3. Fɨ̀fɔ̌d nì ndɔ' bə nì nchɨ̌ mùn.
   - Lɛ bə ŋgâ: Nù yì mùn yɛ̌ ndɨ̌ ù a, à tum bə nì nchɨ̌ mùn.

4. Njɔ̂ŋ-ndab sɔ̀b u, ù ti kwe bə.
   - Lɛ bə ŋgâ: Mùn bi i nì ndab nyin a, bɛ̌ nsuŋ nù nì tù u, a bi.

5. Mô kɨ̀yu' ntɨ̀', ni ndɔb ma mànjì.
   - Lɛ bə ŋgâ: Mon yì, i mà ni nju' ntɨ̀' bə a, bo la' fôn bɔ̂ kù i, ma mànjì.

6. Mbin ŋgə kɔŋni-kɔŋni, bo jà i ntam ma mu'.
   - Lɛ bə ŋgâ: Mùn lɨ̌n mà bɨ̌d nù mbɔ̀ŋkɛd, à tɨ̂' nù mbɨkɛd.

7. Na ù bɛ̌ mbɔ̂ kâ ntɨ̀n, ù jɨ mbo kɨ̀sù' ɛ?
   - Lɛ bə ŋgâ: Mon nì ntəd bə ndìb nǎ i ntɨ̀n a, i bɛ̌ ŋku, yɨ̌ nù mì.

8. Mô-nchi kɨ̌ ndon yɨ̌ ŋgɨ̀ŋ bə nì kə'
   - Lɛ bə ŋgâ: Bon mmǎ mbə ni njɨ, u lìn mô-nchi bə njɔ̂, i kə' a.

9. Ŋkùd kǔd, njɨ bə.
   - Lɛ bə ŋgâ: ŋgàŋ-kǔd (fǎ'fà') mà ni njɨ bə.

1. I am munchinchi (a type of tree): The father of the nation has become valueless.
    - That is; my achievements don't mention of me.

2. You are lucky: you have a bundle of spears behind you.
    - That is: you have many people defending your cause.

3. The storm precedes the rain.
    - That is: what befalls a man is uttered by man.

4. A thorn in the house could be deadly.
    - That is: The enemy in the house is the deadliest enemy.

5. A child who does not heed advice goes astray.
    - That is: Such a child can easily lose his life in society.

6. The cockroach moves slowly but it is caught and thrown into the fire.
    - That is: man can change a good thing to be a bad thing. Good deeds can very easily be construed otherwise.

7. When your mother is living, do you beg for food before eating?
    - That is: A child is proud when his mother is alive. At her death, the child becomes desolate.

8. An Orphan always begs for food by coughing.
    - That is: when children are eating in a group, you can tell an orphan from his cough.

9. A hard worker does not eat.
    - That is: one never reaps the fruits of one's labour.

10. Mû dù yâ̂ tɔŋ.
 • Lɛ bə ŋgâ: Dù yì, à yâ̂ tɔŋ a, nì ŋgə mfuŋ fɛ̀d bi, bo to mbi cho wu' lɛ, nnyɔ̀' i.

11. Mô-ŋkan, nì ntad nchɨm ma lɨ̀', nǎ i chɨm a.
 • Lɛ bə ŋgâ: Nù, nâ mǔn nì nje a, môn ǐ nì nje sɛ̌ bub.

12. Mba ŋgwa' wə̀'nì i bə.
 • Lɛ bə ŋgâ: Nù mùn wa'a, i la' kǔ' yɛ̌.

13. Nchù kɨ̀kam bǎn mfɛd ì.
 • Lɛ bə ŋgâ: Mɔ̌' mùn bɛ̌ ni njɨ, ǎ njaŋ mùn, i mà ni njɨ bə a.

14. Mô-tɔ̌ŋ nda' bə.
 • Lɛ bə ŋgâ: Mô-tɔ̌ŋ mà ni ndə'ni kɨmvi bə.

15. Nyàm mônchi, bo wàd nì ŋgùb.
 • Lɛ bə ŋgâ: Mônchi bɛ̌ ntam nyàm, bǔn ŋgwad bə mbǔ mbù.

16. Wə, mi' yə ni yì ɛ?
 • Lɛ bə ŋgâ: Ŋgàŋ-chɛ̌d-sa' lǐn ŋgâ, i la' ku sɛ̌, bìmɔ̂' bǔn nchɔ'ti sá' yǐ mônchi sɛ̌.

17. Tu masi mɛ'
 • Lɛ bə ŋgâ: Ŋgɔ̀ŋ bùn mɛ' la' ku.

18. Ù bɛ̂ wə mbə̀ vu ɛ?
 • Lɛ bə ŋgâ: Vu mà ndǐn mùn bə.

10. I am the bee that discovers a hive.
    - That is: Such a bee is often killed when the rest of the bees occupy the new home

11. A baby monkey jumps and lands where the mother jumps and lands.
    - That is: One is always a replica of one's forebears. Like father like child.

12. A madman never forgets what he has been doing.
    - That is: A habit is easy to form but hard to break.

13. An empty mouth hates another mouth that is eating.
    - That is: He who does not have, hates those who have (jealousy). He who is destitute hates those living in opulence.

14. A child who loves eating never lives long.
    - That is: A greedy child is very vulnerable to danger

15. An animal shot by an orphan is shared with its skin.
    - That is: An orphan never receives fair treatment in society; An orphan is always treated with levity in society.

16. Wo, can the eye see itself?
    - That is: The Judge knows that at his death, other people shall also judge his orphan's case.

17. All heads are earthbound.
    - That is: Death is the final destination of every human being.

18. Who are you in the face of death?
    - That is: Death is no respecter of persons. Nobody is immortal.

19. Wə nì ŋgə ma môsì bô mùn ɛ?
   - Lɛ bə ŋgâ: Bo nì ntuŋ mùn-ŋgɨ mbə mùn-ŋkə' sɛ̌, masi tâ' tu ì.

20. Ù wàd kǔ-mfòn, ù chî' tù i ya ɛ?
   - Lɛ bə ŋgâ: Bofà mùn-mɔmmɔm tâŋ bèd, kɨ bə̂ mfòn ɛ?

21. Sǐ ndun ŋku bə.
   - Lɛ bə ŋgâ: Kumǔn mà ni ndun majǐ sì bə, kè ŋgâ, mô yum miyǎ nì ŋku ncho bə majǐ bàm.

22. Nchǔ nì njɨ, mi' ŋko-nsɨn.
   - Lɛ bə ŋgâ: Ŋgàŋ-chə̌d-sa' bə̂ njɨ ŋkab ŋkùb mà chə̌d sa', mbə̂ mì' mi tǐ mbɔ' mùn, i jɨ̂ ŋkab sa' mbò i a.

23. Nji mɨ mɛ', ntɔ̆n nǎ i ma mu.'
   - Lɛ bə ŋgâ: Mùn i nì ŋgâ, i lɨ̆n mɛ' a, mbə̂ mùn lɛ kwà' ghɨ̀ghɨ̆n mùn.

24. Kǔjìd bɔ̆ŋ, nji ì bɨ' bə.
   - Lɛ bə ŋgâ: Kǔjìd ŋgàŋ-ŋkab nì njid a, i mà ndɨ̆n mùn kè Nyìkɔ̀b bə, Nyìkɔ̀b bə̂ yi, mfòn kɨ mbə̂ yi.

25. Ntɔ̀ mfêd fed, ndə'ni mà san mbaŋ bə.
   - Lɛ bə ŋgâ: Ù bə̆ njɨ yum, yù kù', ù mà'tì, mbî' bɔ̀m u san.

26. Ŋgu' tìtà bô ŋgu' ndòn.
   - Lɛ bə ŋgâ: Mùn bə̆ njɨ mɔ̆' sa' bə̂ njə̂ i jun a, i bə̂ jɨ bə̂ ndòn.

27. Ndǔ' mfɨnyǔm ndəmɨ bə.
   - Lɛ bə ŋgâ: Ŋgɔ̀ŋ nù mɛ', ù yɛ̆ nì mfɨnyùm a, mà ndɨ̆n mà lèmɨ bi bə.

19. Who goes into the grave with someone else?
    • That is: Both the rich and the poor answer death's call equally.

20. If you cut the Fon's leg, where will you keep his head?
    • That is: A common man cannot plan a war without the fon's consent

21. The grave is never full.
    • That is: a corpse never fills the grave. Nothing is ever too small to put in a bag.

22. The mouth eats while the eye remains shy.
    • That is: when a judge receives a bribe in passing judgment, he carries a guilty face whenever he sees the giver of the bribe.

23. "I-know-all" burnt his mother.
    • That is: anyone who claims to know everything is a big fool. Only a fool claims to know everything.

24. A good journey through life knows not the bad one.
    • That is: a successful man cares less for other people and has little respect for God.

25. Overstuffing easily breaks the pot.
    • That is: too much of anything is a disease.

26. A noble's success is ill-luck.
    • That is: any success achieved through corruption is a curse.

27. Night wine does not hide.
    • That is: Nothing can be hidden under the sun.

28. Ŋgǎ ntuŋ mfòn.
    - Lɛ bə ŋgâ: Ŋgɔ̀ŋ nù mɛ' mǔn nì nchu a, kɛ̀ ya, kɛ̀ ya ɔ, mǔn nì nju'.

29. Ŋgǐn nji mànjì kɔ̀d bə.
    - Lɛ bə ŋgâ: Nù yì, ŋgɛ̀n yě ndǔ ù a, à sûŋ mùn ma ŋgɔ̀ŋ lɛ mbò i.

30. Ŋgɛ̀nyàm tî' chɔ̌bnyàm.
    - Lɛ bə ŋgâ: Mùn-ŋgɨ tî' mùn mɔmmɔm.

31. Bǎ njɨ ŋgɔ̀m, mbɨ nsɛn.
    - Lɛ bə ŋgâ: U nì nchu bɔ̂ yù, yà ka ma ntɨ̀ a ni nto.

32. Nchu'mvi nyin mvɔ̂ bɔ' bə.
    - Lɛ bə ŋgâ: Mɔ̌' mùn bǎ nsuŋ mbɔ̀ wù ŋgâ, bi i ghə njě mɔ̌' nù mbò i, ù suŋ mbɔ̀ mùn lɛ ŋgâ, u nì ŋgə yě yǔ yum sɛ̌ mùn lɛ chû yɔ̀ chu mbɔ̀ wù.

33. Ŋkan ŋgə lentî tu môn ì tìtì, à vù ntəŋ təŋ.
    - Lɛ bə ŋgâ: Mɔ̌' yum mbɔ̀ŋkɛd bǎ ncho mbɔ̀ wù, bò u nì ntɨ̀ u lɔ̀b mɨ̌, ni ŋkiti, ni ŋgə'ni, mbɔ̂ a to bɨ'.

34. Ŋkɔ̀ŋfɨn ŋgə bâm bon, mvǔ chɔ̌dwəd.
    - Lɛ bə ŋgâ: Ù bǎ ni mbam bon, bon bɛ mmà'ti u, ù fətì.

35. Â mbi châ ŋkɔŋnìndàm, i ghâ, i tàm bɔ̂ kɔm.
    - Lɛ be ŋgâ: Tìn ì mà jǐd mà mbə, i ghâ, i jǐd kǔjǐd kɔm.

36. Â mbi châ bà-njì, bo kwe nì ntaŋ.
    - Lɛ bə ŋgâ: Bùn iba bǎ ni nsa' sa', ù jî mùn yì, nù i to bɨ' a, nì njì ì.

28. The Fon's ear is the grass.
    - That is: There is no secrecy in society. Nothing can be kept entirely secret. Even walls have ears.

29. A guest never knows the road to the toilet.
    - That is: whatever a stranger does to you can only be done through the advice of an indigene.

30. The leopard has become a civet cat.
    - That is: a lord has become a commoner.

31. We should eat Ŋgɔm (fruit) while waiting for Mbɨ (another kind of fruit) to ripen.
    - That is: As you talk, expect my own ideas; learn to accept other people's ideas.

32. Mushroom never rots in a day.
    - That is: A single day cannot disrupt all your plans.

33. Mother monkey spoiled the shape of its baby's head because she took too much care in fixing it.
    - That is: Don't overdo a thing.

34. The wasp remained as it is because it spent all the time feeding its children.
    - That is: Don't take care of others and forget yourself.

35. The chameleon claims to walk like a lord when it is unable to walk fast.
    - That is: making virtue of a defect or a vice.

36. When the Njis (kingsmen) fail to execute an errand, they resort to arguments to cover their tracts.
    - That is: When two people are in dispute, the guilty party betrays himself by the tone of his voice

37. Kɨ̀ vi mon, ŋgâ, bo fa i nyɔ'.
   • Lɛ bə ŋgâ: Mùn yì, môn ɨ̌ mà mbə a, bə̌ nju' nù yì mon
   yě a, i ghâ, bo nyɔ̂' mon lɛ̂ nyɔ̌'.

38. Mbûŋ ŋkab, ŋgâ, mɨ̀ŋgwî ndɨ̀m.
   • Lɛ bə ŋgâ: Ŋgàŋ-fɔm nì mfuŋ yûm mbɔ̀ŋkɛd bə nì ì
   mbɨkɛd.

39. Mɨ̌ mbam sɨ̀ŋ, ŋgɔb ŋku.
   • Lɛ bə ŋgâ: Mɨ tɨ̌ njɨ'ti bùn, yǎ bon ŋku njì ɛ?

40. Mbûŋ môn ŋkɨ̌' pìn.
   • Lɛ bə ŋgâ: Ŋgɔ̀ŋ nù mbɨkɛd kɛ̀ sa' nì ncho bə ndû
   mɨ̀ŋgwî kɨ̀ vi mon.

41. Ŋkwin kɔ̀b mmî sɔ̀ŋtì.
   • Lɛ bə ŋgâ: A nì mbə nì lùm, tɨ̂ njamɨ jum ma kɔ̀b, bǔn
   ndɔ' nyin nyin kɛ̀ iba iba, miyà kɔ̀b lan.

42. Mɔ̌' ndɨ̌m ŋgâ, mfɛd ì ɛ, chà'.
   • Lɛ bə ŋgâ: Mɔ̌' ndɨ̌m nì ŋged mfɛd ì yì, i kwêd mùn a,
   ni ŋkwɛd mùn sɛ̌. Kɛ̀ njə̀ghan nì ŋgɨ̂ mfɛd ì yì i jə̌ a, la
   ni njə sɛ̌, à chàmbo.

43. Ndìb à bɔ̌ŋ a.
   • Lɛ bə ŋgâ: Ndìb yì kɛ̌ jam mbə̀ wù a, bǔn bu bə̂ njamɨ,
   ndìb yì, ù fɔm a, bùn bɛ ten u mɛ'.

44. Ŋkùd kǔd mâ ŋgɔb, bo bi jɨ, ŋ-kɔ̌' bə'.
   • Lɛ bə ŋgâ: Mɨ nì ŋkûd yum, bo bi jɨ, ŋgə̀ mà kǔd mɔ̀'.

37. A barren lady says they should give her a child to kill.
   - That is: A barren woman easily prescribes death as punishment for a child.

38. A poor man condemns women to be witches.
   - That is: A poor man hardly appreciates anything good.

39. Feeding the birds of the air and starving the chickens at home.
   - That is: Should one feed strangers and starve one's own children?

40. I longed for a child but conceived a hernia.
   - That is: All blames are directed to a barren woman.

41. Forest firewood has been exhausted through constant use.
   - That is: While little drops of water make a mighty ocean, a forest is depleted little by little.

42. A wizard scandalised by wizardry.
   - That is: a thief scandalised by the act of a fellow thief.

43. When things are good.
   - That is: People come to you when you are rich and run away when you are poor (fair-weather friends).

44. I have done the work of a hen, when it is time to enjoy, I climb into the nest to incubate more eggs.
   - That is: some people are born to toil for others.

45. Mŭn njab yì, nsuŋ yà.
    • Lɛ bə ŋgâ: Nŭ nì mbə ndû mùn, i ləm ni nsuŋ bə ì mɔ̌'
      mùn.

46. Ŋkɔ̌d wi mfǒn, ŋgə̀ tu'kwɛn.
    • Lɛ bə ŋgâ: Wi mfòn bə̌ ŋkɔ̌m ŋkɔ̌d, bo mà'tì yab, ni
      ndab bə̂ ŋkwân yàb.

47. Wə mbi fǎ', mbɛti nsi ɛ?
    • Lɛ bə ŋgâ: Mŭn nì mbi fâ' fà', kɨ̀ bə̂ lîn lɨ̌' ncha' yì, kějɨ̀
      to bɔ̌ŋ fɔ' a bə. Mŭn mà ni nji mɛ' bə.

48. Mfâ' ŋgwà-nyàm, mbim ndɔŋ.
    • Lɛ bə ŋgâ: Ù bə̌ ni mfâ' yŭ fà' bə ma lɨ̌' nyàm, bŭn
      mfuŋ u bə nì ndɔŋ.

49. Ŋkû ŋkŭd mbò ma.
    • Lɛ bə ŋgâ: Kè mùn chɔ̂' ŋkàb u, kɨ̀ fa bə, à tɨ̂' sa' bi i.

50. Mɨ̀ lŭŋ, mɨ̀ ku.
    • Lɛ bə ŋgâ: Ù bə̌ mfuŋ mɔ̌' mùn mà to ŋghèmti u, i to kɨ̀
      lĭn mà ghèmti u bə.

51. Mbɨ̀ŋ kɨ̀ bɔ̌ŋ lɨ̀ŋ.
    • Lɛ bə ŋgâ: Bŭn mà ni mbim bɔ̌ŋ mbɨ̀ŋ bə.

52. Bo suŋ lan, m-bîm bim.
    • Lɛ bə ŋgâ: Bofà n-ti tànì nù bə.

45. Someone leaves his own problems to talk about mine.
   • That is: People don't mind their own business. Leaving the log in your eye and bothering about the speck in another person's eyes.

46. Between the Fon's wives is "ngə̀-tu'kwɛn" (a type of grass).
   • That is: Slaves are punished in place of the Fon's wives who fight. When two elephants fight, it is the grass that suffers.

47. Whoever asks the soil what it can offer before cultivating it?
   • That is: You never can tell what the future holds for you.

48. I work in a barren land and am called a lazy man.
   • That is: A hard worker cannot be identified on a barren piece of land.

49. A good turn begets a loss. I laboured in vain.
   • That is: A creditor who ends in conflict with the debtor.

50. I'm living but I'm dead.
   • That is: When a helper is invited, but cannot really help.

51. Rain has no good name.
   • That is: When it rains, people complain, when it does not, people still complain.

52. I accept all that they say.
   • That is: I never argue – a "yes man."

53. Bà ghə̂ kùd, ŋgăŋ! Bà ghə̂ jɨ; beb a, n-dɔ̂' bàm a.
   • Lɛ ə ŋgâ: Bùn kɔ̆ŋ ma jɨ, nchă mà kŭd.

54. Bɨŋkɨ nì ŋkɔm, vukɛd cho.
   • Lɛ bə ŋgâ: Ghèmti sâ' bɨŋkɨ a ku'ni, mbî' bà bâ yàb to, ŋkɔ̀d tum bà'bà'.

55. Nyâm nsɛ̂n-ŋkwèn, ghăŋ tàm bi jam.
   • Lɛ bə ŋgâ: Mùn bə̆ mvŭ mɔ̆' sa', ghăŋ suŋ făn nù i njam.

56. Mfɨnyàm, vù tam.
   • Lɛ bə ŋgâ: Bɨ̆ nì nchu mɔ̆' nù iba, kè ited, nù lɛ bə̆ ŋgwɛ̆ tâ' mù nyin, fɛ̀d bi mà'tì i nì nù lɛ.

57. Ŋkan kɨ̀fà', ŋkwɛd ndûm lam.
   • Lɛ bə ŋgâ: Mɔ̆' mùn, nì njê mɔ̆' yum, mɔ̆' mŭn njɨ njə̂ ŋkan.

58. Tamɨ ndɔŋ, ù fâ so.
   • Lɛ bə ŋgâ: Ù bə̆ ntă' mà lɨ̆n njə̂ ndɔŋ bə a, ù fâ sofà' mbɔ̀ i.

59. Bo nì ŋkwa'ni ŋgàŋ-làm bə nì ŋki.
   • Lɛ bə ŋgâ: Ù bə̆ ndɨ̆n ŋgâ, ŋgàŋ-lăm to suŋ mbə̆ wù ŋgâ, ŋki-lăm mà mbə mbɔ̀ i bə, ù yə̂ làm mbɔ̀ i, nì mô ŋki-làm.

60. Chi kɨ̀chə', ă nchə' nchàŋ.
   • Lɛ bə ŋgâ: Mùn bofà i yè nù a, mà ni nje bə, à là mùn mɔmmɔm ni njê nù lɛ.

53. "Let's go for work!" "No!" "Let's go and eat!" Wait, let me take my bag."
    • That is: People who prefer food to work. People prefer the easy way out.

54. When children start a problem, elders come in.
    • That is: Elders always intervene in children's problems; It is good to solve children's problems fairly and avoid quarrels among their parents.

55. An animal which turns its back on the hunter has many shooters.
    • That is: The guilty are subjected to a lot of criticism.

56. A blind animal falls into a pit trap.
    • That is: A member of a group is easily forgiven by the group's consent.

57. The monkey which does not work eats the main trap.
    • That is: Someone does little work yet eats like a monkey.

58. Give a hoe and know the lazy.
    • That is: You can tell a lazy fellow by giving him a job.

59. It is with coal that you try a blacksmith.
    • That is: A blacksmith is known by his dirty hands.

60. Nchàŋ (a kind of vegetable) tastes better than salt, which has lost its saltiness.
    • That is: The profane is likely to see what the expert does not.

61. Bà yĕ kɨbɔ̀ŋ, ŋgɔ̆ŋ mbə̀ bo.
    • Lɛ bə ŋgâ: A ni njɨ bùn mbɨkɛd ni njɨ ŋgɔ̀ŋ.

62. Nsə̀nì sə̀ni, mfêd nnɔ̀ŋ nɔ̆ŋ.
    • Lɛ bə ŋgâ: Mùn bə̆ nchi ma kun, mboli miya, mbə̂ miyà
      miyà li we i. Kɛ̀ mùn bə̆ ntasɨ̀' nì nù mbɨkɛd, mbə̂ i to
      yê nù mbɨkɛd lɛ.

63. Li mfêd vu.
    • Lɛ bə ŋgâ: Njə̂ ù li, bùn bì'nì mà ni chuti u a, ù bə̂ kû
      ku bub.

64. Nchĭ ŋgə̂ jìd mɨndŭn i, ŋŋɔti.
    • Lɛ bə ŋgâ: Mùn i nì njid mɨnjɨ̌' i a, mà ndɨn mà yĕ nù à
      chini a bə.

65. Ndàyɨ' ŋgâ, nù cho i, à bə̂ kâ nchàmi.
    • Lɛ bə ŋgâ: Mŭn nì nchu ŋgâ, i nì njə ŋgə', ŋgə' bə̂ ka
      manjàm.

66. Sibô mŭn nì mbi sə̂b mì' mi, mbə̂ fân făn.
    • Lɛ bə ŋgâ: Mùn bə̆ mbubti mɔ̆' yùm i nì bɔ i, mbə̂ i fân
      făn.

67. Kɔ̆'tɨ ti mà mvə̆ bə, bɔ̀' ti tu' bə.
    • Lɛ bə ŋgâ: Ŋgɔ̀ŋ njèninù bu mɛ' ni mbeb nchu' jàŋ u
      kɛ̀ nchu' vù u.

68. Yum, a nì tu chì a, nì tu ŋgab.
    • Lɛ bə ŋgâ: Ŋgə̂' mɨchì bô ì ŋgab bə̆ ŋgə̆ŋŋgə̀ŋ.

69. Mô nchâm cham, nji nsə̆' mànjì bə.
    • Lɛ bə ŋgâ: Mon yì bo cham î cham a, mà ndɨn njə̂
      mànjì bo nì ŋgə a, sə̆' a bə.

61. The world is for evil-doers.
    - That is: The wicked are generally more successful in life.

62. Crawling is a brother to sleeping.
    - That is: A thought is often followed by some action.

63. Sleep is the brother of death.
    - That is: Death is a kind of sleep.

64. The river meanders because it journeys alone.
    - That is: One who is self-centred cannot be objected.

65. Ndayu said he is in trouble when it is just the beginning.
    - That is: Someone who keeps complaining invites more problems.

66. It is an accident when someone pricks his own eye with his finger.
    - That is: More caution is taken when one is dealing with one's affairs.

67. If a tree stump does not decay, mushrooms will not grow on it.
    - That is: Regeneration comes after degeneration.

68. What is on the deer's head is also on the antelope's head.
    - That is: Things that resemble share common problems.

69. A baby who is always carried on the back has no notion of distance.
    - That is: The difficulty is more apparent when you face the problem personally.

70. Nsî Bà'nì kǐ nte bə nì lùm.
    - Lɛ bə ŋgâ: Kɛ̀ ù bɛ̂ mùn-ŋgɨ kɛ̀ ŋkɔm ɔ, à bɔ̆ŋ ù yɛ̀ nù à kù'ni a, nì ndìb ù tî' mùn-ŋgɨ a, kɨ̀ mà'ti ndìb là bə. Kɛ̀ ù ma mbàti ŋgâ, bǔn nì mvû bə nì ndìb mbɨ̀ŋ bə, bo lǐn mà vǔ masi sɛ̆ nì ndìb lùm: Alɛ ù ji'ti ŋgâ, bo ŋkə yǔ nǔ mùn-ŋgɨ mbə̀ wù, mbi' njɔ̂ u mà ndǐn mà yɛ̆ nù mbɔ̀ŋkɛd mǐ a bə.

71. Ŋkɨ̀ bə ndâ ŋgwa' bə, mbə nì ŋkɔŋ chètì.
    - Lɛ bə ŋgâ: Mɨ mà ni mma' bɛ̂ ŋgwa' bə, ù ghâ, ŋ-gabti kɛ̆ ŋgwa' bə mǐ ɛ? – Nù lɛ mà mbə yɛ̆ nù bə, ù suŋ ŋgâ, m-fa bɨ̆dchu bə mǐ ɛ?

72. Yu' mbə̀ bo.
    - Lɛ bə ŋgâ: Mà'ti nǔ bùn, nju' mbə̀ bo.

73. Ndɔ̂ŋ kɔ̀d kɔ̆d, mɛ'.
    - Lɛ bə ŋgâ: Vu, bɛ̂ nù a ndû ŋgɔ̀ŋ bùn mɛ' a.

74. Mâ-mbân mɨ̀njɨ̀' bɔ̆ŋ mà tɔ'.
    - Lɛ bə ŋgâ: Sa' bɛ̆ mbə ndû mfɛd ù, ǔ nchaŋti mà sa'. À bi tî' yù, nsɨn ŋko u mà chu.

75. Bo bɛ̆ nchăb tu mfòn, ù kom.
    - Lɛ bə ŋgâ: U ŋgàŋ tɨ̆n tu.

76. Bo bàn u, mvɨ chetì u nì mu'.
    - Lɛ bə ŋgâ: Bo bɛ̆ mbăn mùn, ŋgɔ̀ŋ kɛ̆ mɔmmɔm mɛ' sɛ̆ mban i.

77. Bo mbu' ndun, i pàd ŋkɛ̆d.
    - Lɛ bə ŋgâ: Yum nì ncho mbə̀ ghɨ̀ghǐn mùn, i ti ji ŋgâ, a yum yì, à bɔ̆ŋ a bə, miyà miyà yum lɛ tum nì bò i.

78. Mâ-ŋgɔb mfu', mfuŋ pɛ̀d-ndab.
    - Lɛ bə ŋgâ: Mâ-ŋgɔb kà sân bòn bi, mbi lɔ̆b mà ni njê kukud, mɨpɛ̀d yu', nto ni ŋgweti bòn bi bɛ.

70. Bali land is only slippery in the dry season.
   - That is: Defend your title or lose it. How the mighty are fallen.

71. I am not in a thrift and loan bank but I have counting sticks.
   - That is: I cannot share what is not mine. I cannot reap where I did not sow.

72. Listen to them.
   - That is: Better to listen to others than meddle in their affairs.

73. The horn that touches all.
   - That is: Death awaits everyone

74. Another man's abscess is easier to incise.
   - That is: It is easy to judge others.

75. If they wet the Fon's head, you can shave it.
   - That is: You are headstrong.

76. If you are hated, a dog will deprive you of basking by the fire.
   - That is: one who is hated is despised even by riff-raffs.

77. They fill a container, he turns it and throws away.
   - That is: A fool does not know the value of anything.

78. A breeding hen attracts the civet cat.
   - That is: You lose your property by trying to take too much care of it.

79. Mâ kun kɨsɨ nì ŋkɨ, nchě nì ì manjàm.
     • Lɛ bə ŋgâ: Mɔ̌' nù bə̌ ni njê mfɛd ù, ù ma ŋgɨ̀ i bə; cham î cham. Miyà miyà, nù lɛ chè ndû ù sɛ̌.

80. Ndìb ŋkà' kǎ mà ŋkɨ a, bo ti mɨ̀ ni ŋkɨ njɨ chɔ̌' ɛ?
     • Lɛ bə ŋgâ: Ndìb yì, mùn kǎ mà ni mfâ'fà' bə a, i ti mɨ̀ ni ŋkɨ nchi ntɨ̀n ɛ? Kɛ̀ i ti mɨ̀ ni ŋkɨ njɨ ŋkab ɛ?

81. Tâ' tu mbàŋ nyin, ndə'ni mà bǎn bə.
     • Lɛ bə ŋgâ: Tâ' mon nyin mà ni ndə'ni mà kǔ' bə.

82. Mɨ lɔ̌' bɔ'tɨ̌ lu'nî mbad mɨ̌ ɛ?
     • Lɛ bə ŋgâ: N-dɔ̌' yǎ yum yì, a miyà a, ŋkù'ti mbə̀ mùn yì, yɨ̌ŋgan njamɨ a ɛ?

83. Bo lòn nyùŋ mbə̀ nyo ɛ?
     • Lɛ bə ŋgâ: Ù lòn yum mbə̀ ŋgàŋ fɔm ɛ?

84. Nchɨ̌ mà'ti kɨ̀ swɨ̌ swɨ̌ bə, ni ŋkɔ' kɔ' ɛ?
     • Lɛ bə ŋgâ: À lɔ̌' ni nto fâ wǔ yum mbə̀ mɨ̀, ù kù' ndon yum bə mbə̀ mɨ̀ ɛ?

85. Ntɔ̀kǔ' ncho nchâm chu'.
     • Lɛ bə ŋgâ: Ntɔ̀kǔ' nì ncho mɨnaŋ ni tu kǔ', mbî' bo nì ndɔ̌' fǔkǔ', ni ntɔb titâ chu' mɨ̌ a.

86. Mì' mu saŋ ɛ?
     • Lɛ bə ŋgâ: Yɔ̀ nù bo nì nje mè a, u ni njə sɛ̌ ɛ?

87. Mbim-nì bim-ni nì nda' ndâ ŋgɔm ì.
     • Lɛ bə ŋgâ: A mà mbǒŋ mà ni mbim ŋgɔ̀ŋ nù mɛ', mǔn nì nchu a bə.

79. The main front bed spring is connected to the hind bed spring.
    - That is: Take care of others' problems, for you may face the same problems too.

80. Were they not eating chɔ' (a kind of fruit) when the hills were not yet set on fire?
    - That is: People still survive with or without a job.

81. A lone cone of palm nuts never takes long to ripen.
    - That is: A lone child matures faster.

82. Can I take the valley to fill up a mountain?
    - That is: Should the poor make the rich richer?

83. Do they borrow hair from a snake?
    - That is: Why go to borrow from the poor?

84. Shall the stream change its course and flow up-stream?
    - That is: Why do you beg from me when I should beg from you instead?

85. The cocoyam shoot betrays achu (fufu made out of cocoyam).
    - That is: What belongs to you is generally what exposes you to danger.

86. Are your eyes open?
    - That is: Are you conscious of what is happening around you?

87. One who accepts all proposals often sleeps in his mother-in-law's house.
    - That is: One should be careful about agreeing with everything people say or demand.

88.   Jɨnì jɨni, ŋkwɛd sâwɔ̀ŋ.
   • Lɛ bə ŋgâ: Ŋgàŋ yə yum njɨ jɨ, la' jɨ̂ dɨ'.

89.   Bo ncha' i, i nju' ntɨ̀ i.
   • Lɛ bə ŋgâ: Mɔ̌' ŋgàŋ-jaŋ, kè mɔ̌' mɨ̀ŋkɨ bŭn nì ncha' i a, a nì nju' yi ma ntɨ̀ i njə̂ tumbùm i bə a.

90.   Mɨtě ŋkə'ti ma nchɨ̌ ntàb i bə.
   • Lɛ bə ŋgâ: U mà ndǐn mà cha' mùn i nɔ̌ŋ ma nchù ndâ ì a bə

91.   Kù' kɨkaŋ tɨ̂' nsûn bɨ̀ŋkɨ
   • Lɛ bə ŋgâ: Mon yì, i mà ni ŋku' ni ndə bə a, bɨ̀ŋkɨ nì ŋkɨ mfuŋ i bə nì ŋkên yàb.

92.   M-fà kə mbàn a, i tà' tù a.
   • Lɛ bə ŋgâ: U bɛ̌ mfa bə̂ kə mbə̀ ŋgàŋ-kɨbăn ù, mbə̂ i nì ŋkɨ nta' bə̂ tù u.

93.   Kɔ̌ŋ kɨ mi'.
   • Lɛ bə ŋgâ: U nì ŋkɔ̀ŋ mùn bə nì mi', ni mban i ma ntɨ̀ u.

94.   U tɨ̌ nda kɨtɨ, mɨ̌ nda masi.
   • Bî mùn bɛ̌ ni nsa' sa', ù suŋ mbə̀ mùn lɛ ŋgâ, ù bɛ̌ ni nda kɨtɨ mà nyɔ̌' a nì fù kè nì lɨ̀m, mbə̂ mɨ tɨ̌ nda yà bə masi mà chà u.

95.   Ù lîŋ nŭ sà', ù lîn ì nì mfɨnyùm ɛ?
   • Lɛ bə ŋgâ: Bŭn nì nsa' sa' nì sà' à bə nì mfɨnyùm, ndɨm kù' nto nì lɨ̀m i, kè fù, ŋkŭ' nsa' sa' lɛ ndɨ̌ ù, mɨ-ndŭn i.

96.   Bo sùm ŋkà', kɨ bu' ɛ?
   • Lɛ bə ŋgâ: Mùn bɛ̌ ndam mɨ̀ŋgwi, i lɨ̌n mà làb i nì mɔ̌' nchu', njə̂ mŭn nì mbu' ŋkà' sɛ̌ a.

88. Gluttony ate a caterpillar.
   - That is: A glutton is more vulnerable to poison.

89. They despise him but he knows his worth.
   - That is: Each person knows his intrinsic values.

90. A rat mole is master in its hole.
   - That is: A person is always more powerful in his dwelling place. Everything is master in his home.

91. Dwarfism renders one a friend of children.
   - That is: children regard dwarfs as their equals.

92. I gave my enemies, but he wanted my head.
   - That is: Your enemy cherishes nothing better than your life no matter how good you are to your enemy he'll want your head.

93. Outward love-untrue love.
   - That is: A wolf in sheepskin.

94. As you fly above, I walk on the ground.
   - That is: when you walk over me, do not poison or bewitch me. I shall walk on the ground and still be proud.

95. You know the things of the day, do you also know the things of the night?
   - That is: Problems are not solved in the same manner by day and by night.

96. Is a drum not meant for beating?
   - That is: A question asked by a husband to his wife. He would love to beat his wife as they beat the drums.

97. U mɨnyî mbôb-ncha'.
   • Lɛ bə ŋgâ: U kwǎ' ŋgàŋ-fɨni-mi'.

98. Ù yu', nì ncha' ma tùŋ-tu.
   • Lɛ bə ŋgâ: Njǝ́ bo nì nsuŋ nù mbǝ̀ wù, ù ti mɨ̀ ni nju'
     bu a bə, u la' yu' nì ncha' ma tùŋ tu, ndìb ù ku a.

99. Bɔ̆ŋ mŭn mbǝ̀ mbom ì.
   • Lɛ bə ŋgâ: A nì njê Nyìkɔ̀b ni njê nŭ mùn, ă mbɔŋ

100. À bôm mbôm a, mbubti a.
   • Lɛ bə ŋgâ: Ŋgɔ̀ŋ nù mbɔ̀ŋkɛd mɛ' mɨ nì nje bì ti mɨ̀ ni
     mbim bə a, lɔ̌' bə mbǝ̀ mùn i kà bom a.

101. Tu, kɨ̀-bɔ̆ŋ nchɔ̀'nì.
   • Lɛ bə ŋgâ: Bŭn mà ni mbim ŋgɔ̀ŋ nù mɛ' yì, u nì nje a
     ŋgâ, à bɔ̆ŋ mɨ bə.

102. Ŋkɨ ntam yǎ nyàm, bo ghâ, mfôn fɔ̆n.
   • Lɛ bə ŋgâ: Ŋgɔ̀ŋ nù mɛ' mɨ nì nje a, bùn ghâ, mɨ mà
     ndĭn nù lɛ bə.

103. A mfòn, mbə nù.
   • Lɛ bə ŋgâ: Mfòn ti mà nnɨŋ mɔ̌' ŋgǝ' ndŭ ù bə, mɔ̌'
     mùn ti lìn mà yě nù ndŭ ù bə.

104. Ù wu' mɛ̀, bô ma mô-sì ɛ?
   • Lɛ bə ŋgâ: Bùn bu njamɨ, bo nɨ nnɨŋ sa' ndû bìmɔ̌' bùn
     kɨmvi; lâ kɨmti ŋgâ, bi à bo mà ni nda' cho nì mô-sì
     nyin bə.

105. Bɔ̆ŋ nna'ti, bɔ̆ŋ mô-ŋkwàn nì kə ɛ?
   • Lɛ bə ŋgâ: Mô ŋkwàn bɔ̆ ŋgu', kɛ̀ ntî' ŋkɔm, bùn
     ŋgɔmti i bə nì mì' mi, ni ŋkɨ mfuŋ i bə nì mô-ŋkwàn.

97. You are a cutlass in dry soil.
   • That is: You are very pretentious.

98. You hear with soil in your ears.
   • That is: A stubborn person refuses to take the advice till his death.

99. A good man is known by his character.
   • That is: It is God who makes one to be good.

100. I am ruined by my creator.
   • That is: All the good things I do and no one accepts come from my creator; an excuse to avoid criticism.

101. A shapeless head.
   • That is: Not all good actions are always praised.

102. Whenever I shoot an animal, people say I have just picked it on the wayside.
   • That is: I am never credited for my achievements.

103. The Fon is what matters.
   • That is: You can only be vulnerable if cursed by the Fon.

104. The grave knows no great persons.
   • That is: You are buried alone no matter how many children you have.

105. Of what importance is pride to a slave child?
   • That is: Your birth determines your place in society. No matter what status he attains, a slave child remains a slave.

26   *CHÛ NNÂNA 202 NÌ CHÛ MÌŊGÂKÀ BÔ JÌŊGLÎSHÌ*

106. Ŋkwàn nsa' la' bǝ.
  • Lɛ bǝ ŋgâ: Mô-ŋkwǎn mà ndǐn mà sa' ŋgɔ̀ŋ bǝ.

107. Mi' ntɨ̀n, bɔ̂' vu tì.
  • Lɛ bǝ ŋgâ: Mǔn nì mbǝ ntɨ̀n ni mbɔ' vu, à bǎ nsǎm bɔ̀ i, i ti kù' mbɔ' bǝ.

108. Njɔŋ mànjǐ nì mbeb ŋgàŋ ì.
  • Lɛ bǝ ŋgâ: Nù mbɨkɛd mǔn nì nje a, nì ŋkɨ mbeb mùn lɛ.

109. Ŋkad kad, mbuŋ ŋgu' bǝ.
  • Lɛ bǝ ŋgâ: Mùn yì, i nì ŋkad kad a, nì mbûm bɔ̀ŋ, ni mbumti boà bɨ' sɛ̌.

110. Fǔ' mǔn, nda i bǝ.
  • Lɛ bǝ ŋgâ: Bofà mùn ti sâm yum yì Nyìkɔ̀b bim ŋgâ, a yǐŋgan a bǝ.

111. Yum mǔn nda i bǝ.
  • Lɛ bǝ ŋgâ: Kɛ̀ a jàŋ u, kɛ̀ vù u ɔ, a nì mbeb u.

112. Ì mǔn mbɔ̀ i, ì mùn mbɔ̀ i.
  • Lɛ bǝ ŋgâ: Yǔ jaŋ ndǔ ù, yà ndǔ mɨ̀.

113. Njǒm mbo mbo.
  • Lɛ bǝ ŋgâ: Mɨ nì nsuŋ yǎ nù bǝ mbǝ̀ Nyìkɔ̀b, ǔ ŋkɨ nsuŋ yù sɛ̌ bǝ mbǝ̀ Nyìkɔ̀b.

114. Njè bɔ̀ŋ, ŋku bɔ̀ŋ.
  • Lɛ bǝ ŋgâ: Ŋ-gǎ mɨ mà lùŋɨ mùn, mùn lɛ wâ' ŋgǝ' lɛ mbǝ̀ mɨ̀.

106. Slave rule shall never be.
   - That is: people of noble birth cannot accept being ruled by a slave child.

107. The eye fears death.
   - That is: Death is feared until it strikes.

108. A thorn on the road waits for its victim.
   - That is: Everybody has his own destiny.

109. A wonderer never lacks a crown.
   - That is: A wanderer meets with good and bad alike.

110. One's luck is always his.
   - That is: One cannot miss what God has kept for him. No one can take the others' luck.

111. One never misses what is meant for him.
   - That is: what is designed by God for you, be it your death or illness.

112. Every man has his own.
   - That is: You have your sickness and I have mine. Everyone has his weaknesses.

113. There are different ways of praying.
   - That is: people have different ways in which they speak to God in prayer.

114. I've done good and died for it.
   - That is: You might end up drowning when saving a man.

115. Mô-ndab mbi kə̂ fù, mfa mbùm ì ŋgâ, bo băn i.
  • Lɛ bə ŋgâ: Mɔ̌' mon i nì nchi majǐ njù' yab a, kà ghə̌ mà kə fù mbɨkɛd mà ni njê yǐ nù mɨ̌; ndìb yǐ fù lɛ kà we i a, i suŋ ŋgâ, yǐ bùn băn i.

116. Ŋgɨm bi ghə̌ mfa mi' mbə̀ wù ɛ?
  • Lɛ bə ŋgâ: U nì njəni mè, mbàti yù bə ŋgâ; ŋgɨm kà bi ghə̌ mfa mi' bə mbə̀ wù, mɔ̌' mùn ti mɨ̀ ni njəni sɛ̌ ɛ?

117. Bɛti ma ndab.
  • Lɛ bə ŋgâ: U nì ŋgâ, bŭn nì nsuŋ nù nì tù u, nù lɛ lɔ̌' bə ma nda ù.

118. Ŋgăm ŋgwɛd mbə̀ mbaŋ.
  • Lɛ bə ŋgâ: Mɔ̌' mùn bə̌ njaŋ, ŋgàm i suŋ ŋgâ, nù ma bɔ̀m i, bo suŋ bub.

119. Nsûn mfŏn tukù'ti
  • Lɛ bə ŋgâ: Mùn bə̌ ni nchi mbə̀ mfòn, mbə̂ mfŏn mà mbə nsun ì bə.

120. Ndab fa u, mvi kə.
  • Lɛ bə ŋgâ: Nù yì, ndâ mùn chu mbi' yi a, mvi mɛ' to bim nù lɛ.

121. Njàm-kɔd nju' nù bə.
  • Lɛ bə ŋgâ: U mà ndǐn mà yu' nù yì, mŭn nì nchu nì tù u njàm-njàm a bə.

122. Nchù u ndun, yă ndun.
  • Lɛ bə ŋgâ: Nù yì, ù tă' mà suŋ mbə̀ mɨ̀ a, yă wu' mà suŋ njam nchă yŭŋgan.

123. Nsɔ̌ŋ ghɨ̌ nji vu bə.
  • Lɛ bə ŋgâ: Bă nì nchi nì ŋgə', ni nsɔbni, lâ bà bə̌ ntaŋ mɔ̌' ŋgàm, nsɔ̀ŋ ghɨ̀ ŋkanyin.

115. A child going in for magical practice offers his life on the pretext that he is hated.
    - That is: There is always an excuse for any bad deed.

116. Since you see so well, do you think the migratory locust on departure gave his eyes to you?
    - That is: a query to someone who claims to be all-seeing.

117. Ask your household.
    - That is: Most troubles originate in the family.

118. Only the pot knows about the palm oil.
    - That is: Internal worries in a patient e.g., a man who has committed suicide.

119. The Fon's friend to his knee.
    - That is: The Fon's servant is not his friend.

120. If the family gives you, the world will take.
    - That is: Whatever is said about a person in his family is accepted by the world.

121. The occiput hears nothing.
    - That is: Gossip about you is usually made behind your back.

122. Your mouth is full, just as mine.
    - That is: You have something to tell me just as I have more to tell you.

123. The smiling teeth know not death.
    - That is: Smiles can still be noticed among mourners.

124. Kŏd-mbèn-ndab mà mbŏŋ bə.
   • Lɛ bə ŋgâ: Bùn lǐn mɨ ŋgâ, nǔ ŋgwèn bə̂ nǔ nsɨn, mfɨni mbɛd a, a nì ndam a, alɛ bo ghâ, mà yě ŋgwèn ma mbèn ù, bɨ' tì.

125. Mŏ' mi' yə̂ yà.
   • Lɛ bə ŋgâ: Mŏ' mǔn nì ŋku, bìmŏ' bǔn nchàŋti, alɛ mùn lǐn mà suŋ ŋgâ, mŏ' mi' yə̂ yà ɛ?

126. Sɔŋ lam mìni nì mu'.
   • Lɛ bə ŋgâ: Kè ŋgə', kè jaŋ, a ndû mùn a, mùn lɛ bim ŋgâ, a mìni mɨ ndǔ i.

127. Yǔ mfòn bə̌ ŋku, ù tûm ntèd.
   • Lɛ bə ŋgâ: Ù bə̌ mbə̂ ŋgwî mfòn, mfòn ku, mbə̂ yǔ nǔ ntèd mǐ mɨ.

128. Mâ-kun bə̌ ŋgâ, ù sǐ mɨ, ŋkə̂ ntàŋ mu ti bə.
   • Lɛ bə ŋgâ: Yǔ mùn bi i nì nchi a, bə̌ nsuŋ nù nì tù u, mùn ti bèd bə.

129. Ù bə̌ mfə' nchǔ ŋgɨ, ù fə' ì tam.
   • Lɛ bə ŋgâ: Ù bə̌ ni ŋka'ni bìmŏ' bon, ǔ ŋka'ni yǔ bon sě bub.

130. Yum, â njê bì a, nì njê ŋga'.
   • Lɛ bə ŋgâ: Bùn bə̌ ni nnɨŋ ŋgə' ndû bì, mbə̂ bo la' nɨŋ ndû nga' sě, mbi' bì bô na', bǎ yàb mɛ' bə̂ kějɨ a.

131. Mâ-mbân mɨ-njɨ̀', bŏŋ mà tɔ'.
   • Lɛ bə ŋgâ: Mǔn nì nchaŋti bə nì nǔ mfɛd ì mà tɔ'ti chɨŋnì i; ni nchaŋti ma ni nchɔ'ti nǔ mfɛd ì, ni ndə̂m yǐŋgan nù mɛ'.

124. A latrine too close to the house is not good.
   • That is: Bad behaviour is not good among neighbours
     e.g., adultery with a neighbour's wife.

125. Somebody's eyes seeing mine.
   • That is: Some people rejoice when people die or some
     people rejoice when another fail in life.

126. The mountain tree is used to wildfire.
   • That is: a patient is used to his regular pains; A hus-
     band (or wife) is used to the behaviour of his wife (or
     her husband).

127. When your Fon dies, leave the Palace.
   • That is: The Fon's wife must leave the palace when
     her husband dies.

128. If the bed complains that you have farted, no one can
    deny it.
   • That is: Your neighbour or a family member is taken
     for his word when he says anything against you.

129. When you blow the mouth of a leopard, you should
    also blow the mouth of a pit trap.
   • That is: When you advise people's children, also do so
     to your own children.

130. What affects kola nut also affects cashew nut.
   • That is: What happens to your neighbour can also
     happen to you. Be sympathetic when others are in
     trouble.

131. Goring someone else's ox.
   • That is: People like to talk ill of other people, hiding
     their poor behaviour.

132. Bo nì nchu nì nchù, ŋgam wa'.
- Lɛ bə ŋgâ: Nù bŭn nì mbati mbi' mùn a, bo bǎ ŋgǎ ŋgam, ŋgam suŋ nù lɛ kwà' ngǎŋŋgèŋ.

133. Mbìŋtǐ nì ntɔ' ŋgùb.
- Lɛ bə ŋgâ: Nǔ nchù u nì nchu miyà miyà a nì mbɨd nti' nù ŋgɨ; nti' kwà' mâ nù.

134. À lâ lǎ bub.
- Lɛ bə ŋgâ: Kè mùn wòŋ u nì fà', kè ndon yum mbè wù, kè mfuŋ û fuŋ, ù ti yè bû ì nyin bə, mùn lɛ lìn nù u kwà' ndani. Ù tǐ' bîm-kɨ yè.

135. Swì kɨtɨ ncho nì bi.
- Lɛ bə ŋgâ: Kè bì fà'fà', kè bì tâm-ndab, kè ìlâ' kùd ɔ, à bi bɔ̂ ndìb, à mǐ a, mɔ̌' mùn cho ŋkanyin, bi à bo jɨ̂ ntàd mi; mbɔ̂ mùn lǐn mà na yɔ̀ chu bub.

136. Bo ncham tɨ̂ njumɨ, à là tɨ̂ mfə mvǔ.
- Lɛ bə ŋgâ: Mɔ̌' mùn nì njaŋ, bŭn mbati ŋgâ, yǐ nù tǐ' vu; mbi chi, mùn ntɨ̀n là ŋku.

137. Ŋkɨndɔ̀ŋ bǒŋ nì ntôm ì.
- Lɛ bə ŋgâ: Mon nì mbɔŋ njɔ̂ nǎ i kâ ntɨ̀n, ni mbeb i a.

138. Mvɨ kɨmu'.
- Lɛ bə ŋgâ: Mon yì nǎ i bɔ́ ba i mà mbə a.

139. Mbɨd kɨ bə.
- Lɛ bə ŋgâ: Mùn lǐn mà bə nì mɔ̌ sa', lâ mùn i lǐn mà bɨd yǔ nù a ti mà mbə, mbɔ̂ ù lǐn mà vǔ sa' lɛ mɔmmɔm.

140. Ŋgɔ' kɨ̌ mbi tum ma nchù, nchàmti.
- Lɛ bə ŋgâ: Bŭn nì mbi yê nù yab, mbɔ̂ taŋ mɨ ŋkuŋ.

132. They speak and the fortune teller confirms.
   - That is: The fortune teller confirms the things people have already discussed.

133. Trapping bursts the skin.
   - That is: Serious quarrels start with little arguments.

134. It is finished just like that.
   - That is: Not being serious; accepting to do a thing and doing it.

135. Descending from a tree to join in a feast.
   - That is: A person who does not participate in a project but comes in during feasting.

136. People sympathise with the dry tree but the fresh tree falls instead.
   - That is: A healthy person dies while the sick one survives. A child dies before his parents.

137. A well-propped plantain grows healthy.
   - That is: A good child is the result of a proper upbringing by his parents.

138. A dog without a master.
   - That is: An orphan.

139. No one to answer.
   - That is: An innocent person who is found guilty because he has no person to speak for him.

140. Termites always confer before coming out of the hole.
   - That is: People always plan before undertaking a project.

141. Bŏm-jɛd, nji bŏm-njì bə.
    - Lɛ bə ŋgâ: Mùn yì, njì jaŋ i a, nì mbi kêŋ njì, mùn i jɨ mɨ njɛd a, ti lìn bî nù lɛ bə.

142. Ntŭ' mŭn tǐ ndun, i ghâ, bo chɨbti chɨbti.
    - Lɛ bə ŋgâ: Bo bɗ ni ngabti yum, kɛ ndù'; mùn ntu' ì lun a, i suŋ mbɗ ŋgàŋ-ghàbti kɗ ŋgâ, bo chɨbti chɨbti; ghàbti miyà miyà.

143. Bo bɗ mfuŋ ŋgɔŋù, mbɗ ŋkà' tɔ' mɨ.
    - Lɛ bə ŋgâ: Ŋgɔŋù bɗ mon. Ba i ti mɨ ni mfuŋ i mbi' kɗjɨ bə, ni ŋkɨ mfuŋ i bə mbi' kùd, kɛ ndìb ŋkà' ì tɔ' a, mà nèbti.

144. Tuŋ ndə ndə, nnànti sa' ni ŋkù mi.
    - Lɛ bə ŋgâ: Mɔ̌' mŭn nì mbi tûŋ mbàb, ntuŋ, nì ndə ndə, alɛ nnăn sa' (=mô bɔ' ŋkə') mbàb nì ŋkù mi, nsam mbàb lɛ.

145. Ŋkɔ̆ŋ ŋgìn, mbăn ntom, ntom jî lɔ'.
    - Lɛ bə ŋgâ: Njɗ u nì ŋkɔ̂ŋ ŋgìn, ni mbân mfɛd ù a, à jî mfɛd ù nji lɔ' a ndŭ ù a.

146. Mô-ŋgɔb kɗ'tikù, kǐ mbɔŋɨ mà cho.
    - Lɛ nə ŋgâ: Ŋgɔb yì, kù i nì njaŋ a, a nì mbi'ni yi ncho, mbi' fɛd bi to mbi taŋni mà cho, nti'ti kù i.

147. Bà mi' yə nu, ù ti kɨ ndəmɨ bə.
    - Lɛ bə ŋgâ: Bìmɔ̆' bɗ ndɗm nù yab, lâ mi' iba kɛ ited bɗ njə nù le, mà lɗm chànì, à tɨ̂' nù sànnsan.

148. Mvɨ nì ŋku nì kən nì tɔ̂ŋ ì.
    - Lɛ bə ŋgâ: Mvɨ bɗ nnyɨ̂' nyàm, mvŭ tam, mbɗ i mà mvŭ bub bə mbi' ba i jìjìd bə, yǐ nù tɔ̆ŋ wu' sɗ; kən bô nyàm.

141. A full stomach knows not the problems of an empty stomach.
   - That is: Those who have may not know how those who have not feel.

142. When someone's cup is full (of wine), he says the others should have only drops.
   - That is: Fortunate people do not always feel for the unfortunate ones.

143. When Ngonu is summoned, then there is work to be done.
   - That is: Society only recognises some people when she needs their services

144. When you dig the hole of a rat mole very fast you miss it.
   - That is: Speed without accuracy.

145. Loving a stranger and hating a brother, but the brother knows every secret.
   - That is: As you love a stranger and hate your brother, it is your brother who knows your weakness.

146. A limping chick comes to roost early in the evening.
   - That is: A chick with a bad leg comes in early, avoiding to be hurt by the healthy ones; prevention is better than cure.

147. When two eyes see you, you can't hide.
   - That is: When a secret is known by two people, it ceases to be a secret.

148. A dog dies with a bone in its throat.
   - That is: A hunting dog does not hunt only for the master, it is also after a share of the game.

149. Nyìkɔ̀b nyam a, ŋgâ i fa a.
- Lɛ bə ŋgâ: Mon mbə̀ wù, kɨ̀ mɨ̀ nju'ni u bə, ù tum i, i ti ghə̀ bə, ù ji nâ yɔ̀ chu lɛ.

150. Bo taŋ kɨ̀ nɨ̀ŋ a, n-nɨ̂ŋ mbùm à ɛ?
- Lɛ bə ŋgâ: Mɔ̌' mùn bə̌ mfuŋ bìmɔ̂' bùn, kɨ̀ fuŋ u bə, mɔ̌' mùn to ŋgâ, bi i ghə wu', ù bèd bu, nsuŋ bub.

151. Mɨ̀ mà mbə vu ku ya bə.
- Lɛ bə ŋgâ: A bùn, bo nì ŋgɔ̂ vu, kɨ̀ lǐn mùn, i ku a bə, bo bà-vu ku ya; ghǎŋ tǎ' ndù', boà nǔ ŋgwèn.

152. Ndǔŋ mbə̀ ŋgɨ̀n, ŋku mbə̀ ntom.
- Lɛ bə ŋgâ: Mùn kɨmvi mà nyɔ̀' u bə, a la' nnyɔ̂' yǔ mùn ì ma ndab.

153. Nsibo nyin, ndɔ̀' ntò ma kɨ̀b bə.
- Lɛ bə ŋgâ: Tâ' mùn nyin ma ndǐn mà yě nù yì, bùn iba lǐn mà yě a bə.

154. Bà kùd ja, bà jɨ̀ ja.
- Lɛ bə ŋgâ: Bà bə̌ ni mfâ'fà' ŋgɔ̀ŋ ì bò mɛ', bim ŋgâ, bà jɨ̀ sě ŋgɔ̀ŋ ì bò mɛ' bub.

155. Mbàn mùn bə̂ vu.
- Lɛ bə ŋgâ: U bə̌ ni mban a kè nì ìlâ' mànjì ɔ, mbə̂ n-dîn yà bə̂ vu yì, à lǐn mà nyɔ' a a.

156. Tɨ̀ ŋku ŋkàm kǎm bə.
- Lɛ bə ŋgâ: Ŋgɔ̀ŋ nù mɛ' bɨ̌ nì mbom nì tù a a, mà ndǐn mà nyɔ̀' a bə.

157. Mɨ̀chɨ̌ ŋgâ, i yu' bə nì ŋgùb.
- Lɛ bə ŋgâ: Mɨ̀ nì nti' nju'ti bə nì mbùm à, njə̂ kɔ̀ŋ u, kè ndìkàŋ ù cho ndǔ mɨ̀ a.

149. God deprived me, saying he gave me.
  • That is: Proverb to a disobedient child.

150. Do I invite myself when I have been left out?
  • That is: Avoid being an unwanted guest.

151. I am not a deathmonger.
  • That is: People who go to death celebrations without knowing the dead, they go for wine and women.

152. I am safer with strangers than with family members.
  • That is: Your source of death is more from within the family than from without.

153. One finger cannot take a piece of meat from the dish.
  • That is: One person cannot accomplish what two persons can accomplish.

154. If we work together, we should also eat together.
  • That is: Collective sharing of the fruits of a collective endeavour.

155. Only death hates people.
  • That is: No amount of hatred can kill a man. Only death can.

156. A tree full of skinned barks does not easily die.
  • That is: All bad things said about a person do not kill him.

157. The deer says hears with his skin.
  • That is: Until your bullet or spear pierces my skin, then would I feel the impact of your action.

158. Kɨ̀ nǔ wə ɛ?
  • Lɛ bə ŋgâ: Nǔ mà ŋkǎm ndû tâ' mùn nyin bə.

159. Mɨsɨ̂ŋ ŋgâ tɨ ɛ, ù lɔ̌' mbi bɛn, i nti' ŋgɔ̂ ghǎ.
  • Lɛ bə ŋgâ: Ù bi nyɨ̀' a, yǎ ndìb mà ghǎ bɔ̂ kǔ' mɨ.

160. Fobà nchi' ŋkab, njàŋ bàm kàm i.
  • Lɛ bə ŋgâ: Bofà mùn ti lìn mà chi' ŋgɔ̀ŋ kě mɛ' bə.

161. Mbɔ̌ŋ mi bə.
  • Lɛ bə ŋgâ: Yum mbɔ̀ŋkɛd mà ni nda' mǐ bə; mɨ̀ŋgwi kɛ̀
    ŋkab.

162. Chə'kêd chi mbə̀ ndâwə, i la' njì ɛ?
  • Lɛ bə ŋgâ: Ŋgwi ù bə̌ mbɔ̂ mɨ̀ŋgwî mbɨkɛd, mbɔ̂ bofà
    ù ti lâ' njì njɔ̂ ŋkə̀ bə.

163. Mɨ̀ŋgwi kɨ̀ vi, yàyà ŋgònŋgòn.
  • Lɛ bə ŋgâ: Mɨ̀ŋgwi kɨ̀ vi, kɨ mbɔ̂ ŋgònŋgòn nì ŋgɔ̀ŋ lùm
    i mɛ'.

164. Nchù bɔ̂ ked.
  • Lɛ bə ŋgâ: Nù, à tum ma nchù a, ghǎ mɨ, bofà ù ti wè
    mɔ̌'ŋka bə.

165. Bùn bɔ̌ŋ-ntɨ̀n.
  • Lɛ bə ŋgâ: Mǔn nì mbə ntɨ̀n, bô nsun ǐ ŋkad, ndìb i vû
    jaŋ a, nsun ì lɛ wa' i.

166. Sun bì ntɨ̀n, to njə bì ŋku.
  • Lɛ bə ŋgâ: À bɔ̌ŋ bùn bo nì ŋkani a, to njə ì lɛ, i nì njaŋ
    a, njɔ̂ bo wa' i a.

158. Who has no problem in the world?
- That is: No one is free from problems

159. The bird tells a branch; before you broke, I was already flying away.
- That is: Before you sent me away, my departure time had come.

160. Foba saves a lot of money, but lacks a needle.
- That is: No one can have everything in the world.

161. Goodness or kindness is timeless.
- That is: Goodness or kindness never finishes.

162. Who has ever slept hungry while having salt in the kitchen?
- That is: No matter how wicked your wife may be, she will provide you with food.

163. A barren woman is always a girl.
- That is: A barren woman always looks young, in spite of her age.

164. The mouth is an arrow.
- That is: A thing said can never be withdrawn. What comes of the mouth cannot be withheld.

165. Man is good alive.
- That is: A well-to-do person has friends, but when encountering misfortune, then all abandon him.

166. Friends in good health should see him (a patient) before he dies.
- That is: Friends who are still enjoying life should visit the sick friend and see how he has been abandoned.

167. Nchi' nì bò a, ni nti' ndɔ' bə nì kɔ'tàŋ.
  • Lɛ bə ŋgâ: Yum bɛ̂ yǎŋgan, m-bi lɔ̌', mùn ti kɨ̀ mbim mà fa mɨ̀ bə.

168. Ntum nì njàm à, nda' mfə'.
  • Lɛ bə ŋgâ: Mùn lôn mɨnyi mbə̀ wù, kɨ̀ fa bə, ù tà' yum wâd yum mɨ̌ kɨkaŋ.

169. Wùmtì nì tù a, mbɨ̌ŋ ndo a.
  • Lɛ bə ŋgâ: Mon mbə̀ wù, ŭ ntâ̂' mùn u tum i a, kɨ̀ yə bə.

170. Bamtì nì bò a, mu' nton a.
  • Lɛ bə ŋgâ: U bə nì bùn njamɨ bì, bofà bo ghèmtì u a, lâ nù njamɨ ŋkɨ ncha û chǎ.

171. Mɨ nì ndù' bə, ŋkɨ nno yà bɛ̂ ləŋni kam.
  • Lɛ bə ŋgâ: I kɨ̌ mà ni nno ndù' bə, ni nno yì bɛ̂ nchì.

172. Ŋ-gǎ nì kɔ̀ŋ ŋkwe nì mfam.
  • Lɛ bə ŋgâ: Mùn ghɛ̂ bèd kɛ̀ ma ndâ-jaŋ, ŋku, à ti' mbɨni kɛ̌ bi.

173. Li bɛ̂ ŋgam.
  • Lɛ bə ŋgâ: Njɛ̂ ù li a, bɛ̂ lì'mɨ̌ vu, ù kù' ni mfuŋ ŋgam mbi' kə ɛ?
  • Li na'ti mɨ njɛ̂ u la' ku a, mbə̀ wù.

167. I kept something within reach but now I need a ladder to take it.
   - That is: Being deprived of something that belongs to you.

168. I go out with my axe but sleep in a cold house.
   - That is: Someone borrows your axe and you have nothing with which to fetch firewood.

169. I have an umbrella, and rain is falling on me.
   - That is: You have a child but lack someone to send on an errand.

170. I have a pair of tones yet fire burns (hurts) me.
   - That is: You have many people to help you, yet problems overwhelm you.

171. I don't have palm wine, but only drink dirty brown water.
   - That is: He does not drink palm wine but only drinks water.

172. I went out with a spear but came back with the handle.
   - That is: Someone went to war or hospital and came back dead, or only his belongings were brought back home.

173. Sleep is an oracle.
   - That is: Sleep is a manner of death. Sleep indicates a pattern of death.

174. Chi chǐ' a ŋgâ, mɨ la' ku və.
   - Lɛ bə ŋgâ: Nchibàŋ i suŋ mbò i ŋgâ, i la' ku, kɨ yə ŋkû ba i bə.

175. Ŋgam nì ŋgwad i.
   - Lɛ bə ŋgâ: Mǔn nì nsuŋ bə̂ nù i lǐn a.

176. Ntân mǔn mì' mi.
   - Lɛ bə ŋgâ: Mi' mǔn nì nna'ti yum à bǒŋ i a.

177. Sòŋ chɔ', bo wâ' lɨm ɛ?
   - Lɛ bə ŋgâ: Sǒŋ mùn bə̌ nchɔ', mbə̂ bofà i ti wâ' lìmti bə.

178. Mfǒn nyad, bɨ bə̂ ndòŋ mi.
   - Lɛ bə ŋgâ: Bùn bə̂ kǒŋ mfòn, mbə ndìkàŋ ì sɛ̌.

179. Tam nnya' mànjì.
   - Lɛ bə ŋgâ: Nnya' yì, a ma mànjì a, bùn mɛ' nì ŋkwɛd.

180. Ŋkù kə̂ mànjì tâm, kɨ bə̂ bǎ' ghə̀ ɛ?
   - Lɛ bə ŋgâ: N-jê nù lɛ, kè m-fâ'fà' lɛ mbi'kə. Yǎ yum ti bə wu' ɛ?

181. Nyo kɨ num bə̂ bà mô-ntâ-saŋ, ghǎŋ bi nyo.
   - Lɛ bə ŋgâ: Sa', kè ŋgə', kè vu nì ŋkɨ ncho bə ndû bùn bì, bo lîn chìŋni nù lɛ a.

182. Sibo lɔ̀b ma chìŋnì tìtì, à ti lə'nì mà ta' mbɛd bə.
   - Lɛ bə ŋgâ: Ù ti mà ni ŋgwê mbùm ù bə, ù ti lə'nì mà fǎn nù bə.

174. A blood sign tells me that I shall die and miss my way.
   - That is: His blood told him that he shall die without seeing his father's corpse: he shall die before his father.

175. The oracle is against him.
   - That is: One only says what he knows, the truth.

176. Man's luck is his eyes.
   - That is: The eye seeks that which is good.

177. When the teeth all fall off do we throw away the tongue?
   - That is: One's tongue is still useful even in a toothless mouth.

178. The Fon is a buffalo and we are his horns.
   - That is: The Fon's people are his guns and spears; with his people.

179. A roadside garden egg.
   - That is: Everybody can eat garden eggs that grow along the roadside.

180. The foot has taken Tam's road but cannot go further.
   - That is: I have done the work with no personal benefit in it.

181. Snakes always bit snake charmers.
   - That is: Many people know the sources of their problems: death, illness, court cases, troubles etc.

182. When a finger remains too long in the anus, it easily becomes messy.
   - That is: you can easily go wrong if you are not patient.

183. Bo ji a ndab, ŋkɔ̂ŋ à ti ku' mbə.
   • Lɛ bə ŋgâ: Lîŋ mbɨkɛd bə̂ mbì'ni ntum mbi' wù ma yǔ ŋgə̂d, mbə̂ mù kɨmvi mà ndǐn mà kǔ' ŋkɔ̂ŋ u bə.

184. Jǎ-njǐ nì ndɔ' bə ma ndab.
   • Lɛ bə ŋgâ: Wɔmtǐ mǔn nì ndɔ' bə ma nda ì, mvi ji wɔmti mùn.

185. Bà kɨ lun, à chə̀d ŋkɨ̌ bàm.
   • Lɛ bə ŋgâ: Yum mà njam bə, bo ndon lon mbə̂ mɨ.

186. Ndôn lon, mvɨ cham.
   • Lɛ bə ŋgâ: Ù lôn mɔ̌' yum, bo kǔ' ŋkə mbə̂ wù mɛ'.

187. Mfə̂kǔ ŋgâ, mɔ̌' njid a.
   • Lɛ bə ŋgâ: Mfə̂kù kà ghâ, mɔ̌' ba' nto.

188. Ŋkôm-ŋkà' ku, bo kə̀ŋ i nì tɔŋ lə'.
   • Lɛ bə ŋgâ: Mùn i nì njê nù mbɔ̀ŋkɛd a, ŋgə' nì mbi chà i, mùn mà ghèmti i ti bə. Kè mùn i nì ŋkom-ŋkà' a, nì ŋkom ni mfinti mɛ', bo tà' mɔ̌' mà bu' ma lɨ̌' vù i kɨkaŋ.

189. Ŋkòn-ŋkà' ù, jâm tà tì.
   • Lɛ bə ŋgâ: Nù bu jam tì, kè ù kwètî nù tì.

190. U nchǐ fǔkǔ' ɛ?
   • Lɛ bə ŋgâ: Fǔkǔ' nì ndeti nchì, ŋkɨ̌d nchì lɛ nì chɨ̀ŋni mfɛd ì, yǐŋgan njum.

191. N-tum mɨ ma kɔ̌b ndù' kɨ wɔ̌b, ŋgɔ̌b ma ndab.
   • Lɛ bə ŋgâ: Ù châm yùm u ma ŋgwɛn, mbi chě ma ndab, bǔn ntaŋni.

183. A conspiracy in the household results in the loss of one's good name.
   - That is: if you have a bad name in the family, the world will no longer love you.

184. All praises start from the house.
   - That is: Respect for a person starts with his family before others can respect him.

185. The bag is not full, yet its strap is giving way.
   - That is: I do not have enough for myself but everybody is borrowing, even the little I have.

186. What I borrowed, the dog has carried away.
   - That is: They have taken everything I borrowed from them.

187. Mfə̂kù commands a leg to move.
   - That is: A lazy leg said another leg is coming.

188. A drum carver dies and only a horn is used for his death celebration.
   - That is: A man who does good to others always lacks a helper in times of need.

189. Your hill has lots of grasshoppers.
   - That is: your problems are many.

190. Are you water in a cocoyam leaf?
   - That is: you are kind to other people but show no kindness to family members.

191. I came out of the palm bush without entangling myself, only to return home and get entangled.
   - That is: Everyone is scrambling over what you alone brought from the farm.

192. Ndɔ̌' mɨ ndə̀ŋ u, nnăn sèn.
   - Lɛ bə ŋgâ: Wo-ŋgɨ̌ŋ ǎ wu', mà ləm ŋgɨ̀ŋ, bǔn mbi lâm ŋgɨ̀ŋ mà lam, mɨ nti' nnaŋ yǎ ŋgɨ̀ŋ bə̂ ŋgwàfɨd.

193. Njɔŋ ì, ì bǔn foŋguŋ a.
   - Lɛ bə ngâ: Bèd ba' mbə̂ bùmti mɨ ma ŋgwɛn ɛ?

194. Bo yě ni njə.
   - Lɛ bə ŋgâ: Bo ji mɨ nù lɛ, bo nì nje a.

195. Mi' wə mà mbə ɛ?
   - Lɛ bə ŋgâ: Mi' ŋgò̀ŋ bùn mɛ' wu', ni njə nù mbɨkɛd mɛ' a nì nda majɔ̂' bùn a.

196. M-bə nì ŋkɔ̀ŋ, kɛ̀ nì ghɨb ɛ?
   - Lɛ bə ŋgâ: Yǎ kə mɨ̌ ɛ?

197. Ŋgɨ̀ŋ ma ntòn u, u led ŋkù bə.
   - Lɛ bə ŋgâ: À bə̌ nchà u, ù ma ntǎ' mɔ̌' mùn ì njɨ̌' bə.

198. Bà ŋkù u ka ni ncham u.
   - Lɛ bə ŋgâ: Njə̂ ŋkù mu iba kâ ntɨn, ǔ njid mɨ̌ a, u ma ndɨn ŋgə' kɛ̀ jaŋ, a to wè u a bə, lâ ti' njid ni nji'ti.

199. Chɨ̀chwè bɨ̀ŋɨ̀, nnya' jam.
   - - Lɛ bə ŋgâ: U nì mbɔ' mi' mùn mà yě mɔ̌' nù, ndìb yì mùn lɛ kɨ̀ bə a, ù bə nì tɨ̀n mà yě nù lɛ.

200. Ma ŋgwě ŋgɔb nì nchu' ntòntŏn bə.
   - Lɛ bə ŋgâ: Ù bə̌ ni mbati mà yě mɔ̌' yum, ù bɔ̀ŋɨ̀ mà chù'ti yù.

192. I have blocked a hole with your bamboo.
  - That is: I eat corn instead of fufu, although I have a grinding stone.

193. Its thorn which lacks fongun.
  - That is: Is war about to start in the farm?

194. They see what they do.
  - That is: Deliberate action.

195. Who has no eyes?
  - That is: People all have eyes that see the bad things that happen amongst men.

196. Do I have a spoon or a ladle?
  - That is: What is my business in the matter?

197. Don't complain about the coldness of the gumbo when it is hot.
  - That is: When you cannot handle a matter, do not blame someone else.

198. You are still on your two legs.
  - That is: Be careful in all that you do while you are still straight, young and healthy, for you cannot tell what trouble or illness may befall you.

199. The caterpillar has gone, so garden eggs will bear.
  - That is: When the master is away, everyone becomes a lord; when the cat is away, the mouse can dance.

200. Do not catch a fowl on the day of roasting.
  - That is: Always plan ahead of time.

201. A nì ŋkɨbti ndaŋ, à ti kὺ' ndun bə.
   - Lɛ bə ŋgâ: Bǔn ni ŋkɨbti màd yàb njâm bìmɔ̂' swè'ti -nù.

202. Ŋgàm kà bôŋ ghan, i ghɨ ma ntăb ŋgwàfɨd.
   - Lɛ bə ŋgâ: Mɔ̌' nù, ù kǎ ndə̂m lɛ̆m a, ŋgàm kà bɔ̀ŋ u, ù tɔ̂' nù lɛ nì tumbùm u.

201. When the container changes, the volume reduces.
   • That is: Attitudes change with changing circumstances.

202. The conversation so amused a corn thief that he laughed in the granary.
   • That is: When a conversation is very exciting, one can reveal his secret.

ABOUT THE AUTHOR

The name Alfred Willibroad Daiga immediately conjures the picture of a politician. A politician he was, an honourable member of the West Cameroon House of Assembly representing the Bali constituency under the Kamerun National Democratic Party, K.N.D.P. banner from 1961. He later became secretary of State for Local Government.

But he was a lot more than that. A few of his contemporaries might recall that he was a constable in the Nigerian Police Force (N.P.F), Secretary of the West Cameroon House of Chiefs and a self-made but accomplished photographer. Although ill-fated and ill-equipped, he was a daring and determined mission-ary, explorer in desolate and hostile fields latent with potent underground priceless ores. He undertook the thankless task of clearing the quagmire till he struck a vein of ore, then he had just the time to place a pointer and move on to the next excavation spot, hoping that future better-equipped professionals in the field would deign to follow his footstep on the quicksand of time and polish the crude oxide into gleaming precious metals.

One of the fields he explored was that of recording oral history in all its forms. In fact, he championed the creation of the Bali Historical and Cultural Committee. And as an aside, he collected 202 proverbs in Mungaka. We cannot tag a date to that collection because it was a long and arduous process. But we remember carrying his tape recorder to the late Ba Tita Langa's compound for that purpose in June of 1963. The old man was barely audible. It took many sessions. We also remember that some of them were told by late Ba Pastor Ndifon whose preaching at the Ntanfoang Presbyterian church used to move mountains.

It is rather frustrating for us to be unable to date these proverbs when one remembers that he was a careful chronicler who documented many events by notes and photographs that carried the time, day and year. As secretary of numerous institutions and associations, he produced enormous pages of dated and meticulously collected relics and mementoes. Ironically, we know little about him. The scarcity of his person is nothing less than a tribute to his self-effacement.

Since this is not and cannot be a biography of the man, we leave that future skilled writer to sift the wealth of data he left behind and hew from the coherent one. However, it is necessary to state that A. W. Daiga was born during the groundnut harvesting season of 1922 in Bali Nyonga, a city-state in the Grassfields region. By the time he was ready for school, the British were in command of the territory. He started with the vernacular school and continued his primary school in Mbengwi and then proceeded to Bonjongo, being one of the pioneer students of Sasse College. He then got recruited into the Nigerian police force after training in Maiduguri. He left the police force shortly after and did full-time farming and animal husbandry in Bali. During this time, he offered his services to the Fon of Bali, created the Bali tourism board, introduced the credit union and got elected councillor on an independent ticket. As a parliamentarian, he attended a course on local government at the University of Birmingham.

His benevolent and humanitarian services also included the funding of the scholarship board and the creating of the Bali Social Club. Some of his charitable endeavours were so intimate and touching. We can still hear the rantings of his godson, who had gone mental and rejected by his blood family. Our father took him into our house with his chains. Another case was that of a distant uncle who suffered from tuberculosis; a former CDC plantation worker, he was abandoned by his wife and children in Tiko. He went and took him to live with us till his death many years after from that terrible disease.

On the 22nd of July 1967, he wrote a circular letter to his "Brother and Sisters", introducing to them some scripts that he had sent to Radio Buea:

1) "A brief history and location of Bali"

2) "The Lela dance"

In that letter he said, "I did this in order that we should not miss the opportunity and with the understanding and confidence that you and our traditional authorities are behind me to replace these sketchy notes with the comprehensive detailed ones as soon as I refer the matter to you.

I am therefore referring the matter to you here and now for the appropriate action…"

We are sure that if he had to publish "202 Proverbs in Mungaka," he would have said the same thing.

A.W. Daiga was married and had eight children, two of whom died in childhood. The six and his widow have survived him since his departure on the 7th of July 1972.

Bengyela & Dinga Daiga

INDEX

mountain xi, 21, 31
mouse 47
mouth 5, 7, 29, 31, 39, 43
mushrooms 9, 17

nation 3
needle 39
neighbour xviii, 31
night 23

oracle 41, 43
orphan 3, 5, 33

palace xvii, 31
palm bush 45
palm oil ix, 29
patient xviii, 29, 31, 39, 43
plantain 33
poison 23
poor, the 7, 11, 21, 31
problems 13, 15, 17, 21, 35, 39, 41,
        43, 45

rain 3, 41
rat mole 23, 35
relics 52
river 17
roadside 43

salt 15, 39
secrecy 9
secret 9, 35, 49
sickness 27
slave 25, 27
Slaves 13

sleep 17, 41
snake 21, 43
society ix, 3, 5, 9, 25
soil 13, 25
spear 37, 41
stomach 35
stranger 9, 35
suicide 29

Termites 33
thief 11, 49
time x, xv, xvi, xvii, xviii, xix, xx,
        xxi, 9, 11, 39, 47, 51, 52
toilet 9
tongue 43
tourism 52
traditional authorities 53
tree 3, 17, 31, 33, 37
trouble 17, 31, 47

umbrella 41

valley 21
values x, 23
vegetable 15
virtue 9

war 7, 41, 47
water 11, 41, 45
wife xv, 23, 31, 39, 53
wildfire 31
wine 7, 35, 37, 41
witches 11
wizardry 11
women 11, 37
worker 3, 13, 53

Y

young xvi, xxi, 39, 47, 61

ABOUT THE PUBLISHER

Spears Books is an independent publisher dedicated to providing innovative publication strategies with emphasis on African/Africana stories and perspectives. As a platform for alternative voices, we prioritize the accessibility and affordability of our titles in order to ensure that relevant and often marginal voices are represented at the global marketplace of ideas. Our titles – poetry, fiction, narrative nonfiction, memoirs, reference, travel writing, African languages, and young people's literature – aim to bring African worldviews closer to diverse readers. Our titles are distributed in paperback and electronic formats globally by African Books Collective.

Connect with Us: Go to www.spearsbooks.org to learn about exclusive previews and read excerpts of new books, find detailed information on our titles, authors, subject area books, and special discounts.

Subscribe to our Free Newsletter: Be amongst the first to hear about our newest publications, special discount offers, news about bestsellers, author interviews, coupons and more! Subscribe to our newsletter by visiting www.spearsbooks.org

Quantity Discounts: Spears Books are available at quantity discounts for orders of ten or more copies. Contact Spears Books at orders@spearsmedia.com.

Host a Reading Group: Learn more about how to host a reading group on our website at www.spearsbooks.org

www.ingramcontent.com/pod-product-compliance
Lightning Source LLC
Chambersburg PA
CBHW022144090426
42742CB00010B/1386